RObbErs BoNEs & Mean DOgS

ROBBeRS

Bones & Mean Dogs

compiled by BARRY AND VELMA BERKEY

drawings by Marylin Hafner

Addison-Wesley

Addison-Wesley Publishing Company, Inc.
Reading, Massachusetts 01867
Printed in the United States of America
ABCDEFGHIJK-WZ-798

Book designed by Charles Mikolaycak

Library of Congress Cataloging in Publication Data

Main entry under title:
Robbers, bones, and mean dogs.
  SUMMARY: Children express their fears in their own
words.
    1. Fear — Juvenile literature. [1.   Fear]
I.   Berkey, Barry R.   II.   Berkey, Velma A.
III.   Hafner, Marylin.
BF575.F2R58   152.4   77-10727
ISBN 0-201-00570-0

To our children,
KENT, RICHARD, and LORI

I'm afraid of floods and very tight places. I feel almost sick in my stomach and my legs won't move. My legs just turn to rubber. I get very nervous. And when I'm in very tight places I feel I have to have air.

I am really afraid of elevators. I just can't get on one without holding someone's hand. Once my grandmother and I got on one when I was only 7 and we fell. I fell all the way down on

the up elevator and got my foot and arm caught. They had to stop the elevator and get some tools to pry me out. That's why I am afraid of them.

I am a little bit afraid of spiders and snakes. This may seem a little bit funny but I am also a bit afraid of elephants in the zoo because last time I got near one it squirted me!

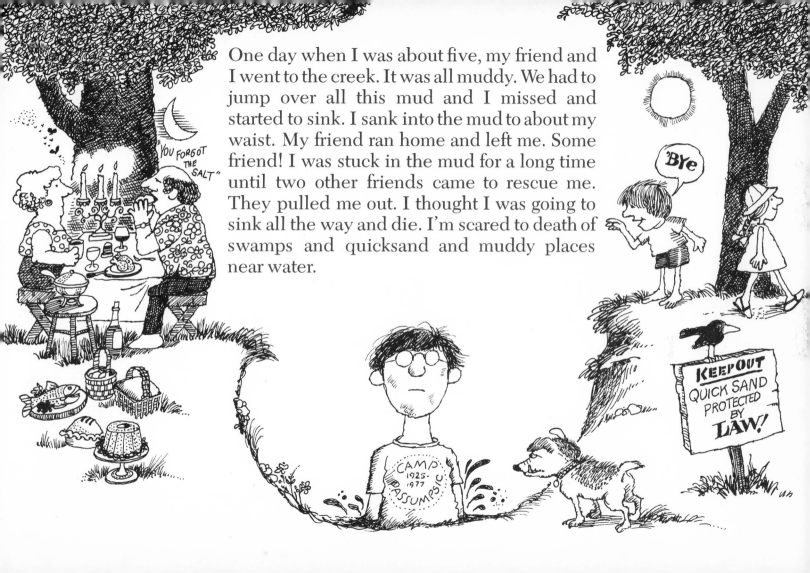

One day when I was about five, my friend and I went to the creek. It was all muddy. We had to jump over all this mud and I missed and started to sink. I sank into the mud to about my waist. My friend ran home and left me. Some friend! I was stuck in the mud for a long time until two other friends came to rescue me. They pulled me out. I thought I was going to sink all the way and die. I'm scared to death of swamps and quicksand and muddy places near water.

I am afraid of silence. I realized it when I was eight. One night my mom and dad did not say anything to each other and I got scared and could not go to sleep. They were mad in their silence.

I'm afraid of slamming doors. Because when I was about two years old my sister shut the door on my finger. So I went to the doctor. My mom said that if I had another doctor, I probably wouldn't have my finger. But this doctor was real nice because she cared. So she stitched up my finger and I am grateful to her.

Now I am not so scared because I am more careful I hope! But I am still not quite over slamming doors.

I am afraid of a murderer coming into my bedroom and choking me to death. Because then I would not be able to play with my friends any more. I would not be able to go to Ben Franklin, my favorite store, and buy stuff. I would not be able to ride my three speed bike any more. I would not be able to read a book or color with crayons. But I would be able to sit in the ground and be dead.

One of my private things is that I'm scared of talking to boys that I like. I get kind of embarrassed.

Whenever I come out of the bathroom I run past the coat closet because I think something is in there. I'm afraid of most dogs because the dogs I know have big teeth and they charge at you when you get close.

I am afraid of my Dad when I do something bad. And I run to my Mom, and then Mom gets mad. And I run to my cat, but my cat scratches me. And then I run to my treehouse and then I get splinters in me. Then I cry.

When the teacher called on me to talk in front of the class, I panicked. I couldn't remember what I was supposed to say. I got so scared that I wet my pants. I felt ashamed and embarrassed. The teacher told me to go to the bathroom and she came in to talk to me. She calmed me down.

I fear staying home alone because I think someone is going to come into our house. I think this because we were robbed two times last year. I imagine hearing creaks and voices. If I have to go upstairs, I take my cat with me. I am afraid of being out at night. Robbers. Bones. Mean Dogs. Electric wires. Dying. Being shocked.

I am afraid of the dark because when I'm in bed I hear the curtains flutter. They sound like ghosts laughing at me. My coatrack looks like a skeleton with some of its skin hanging.

When I am in bed and afraid at night, I start talking to my brother to see if he is there. Even if he yells, "Don't bug me. I'm trying to sleep," I feel better. Talking to him helps because then I know he's there.

I am sort of afraid to talk to some grown-ups.

When I am afraid, I feel shaky and whirly. I feel like I am a bit more heavy inside.

I'm afraid of black widows, tarantulas and snakes. Especially the most poisonous ones.

Sometimes I think that someone is under my bed and sometimes it sounds like someone is behind the picture on my wall.

When I stand up and do something in front of new people I feel very unhappy and I don't feel like I am a person any more.

I fear wasps because I had a bad experience. When I was in fourth grade, we were playing outside for break. All of a sudden this wasp came and started buzzing around me. I flapped my hands at it and then ignored it. But all of a sudden, it came down on me and stung me. I let out a yell of agony. Everyone came over to see why I screamed. A teacher took me to the office to get it fixed up. Ever since then, if a wasp comes around, I go running.

GOTCHA!

DANGER
BIG
HOLE

Four years ago I fell fifteen feet into a pit and lost my breath. My friend jumped in to help me out. When I finally caught my breath, I got out of the pit. I had cuts on my chin and above my right eye. He took me home and my mother patched me up. I was afraid of big holes after that and I still am.

I fear that this year will be the worst year of my life because in fiction and in a true life book I have read something bad happens to a boy when he is ten. I don't know what, but it will be bad.

I am afraid to get in fights. I don't like fights. Especially with a mean bully. Because, if he's bigger than I am, I might get a black eye.

Last summer my Mom and Dad took me with them to Texas on a vacation. I didn't want to go. I hated it. I felt a scarey feeling but it wasn't scarey-scarey. It was this sick feeling in my stomach. My mom and dad took me to a doctor. He checked me over. He told them I was nervous. They didn't know what the doctor meant. But I did. And he was right, too.

I know someone is trying to kill me. I just know it. One day it will catch up to me. It is watching me right now! My mom or dad do not know what I go through.

The first thing I am afraid of is my dad. Whenever my teacher calls my dad he always yells at me. He says I better not get any more phone calls or notes sent home. Then he says, if I do, I will spank you.

If I have to go in water over my head I start to cry. I never never go near a lake or pond or ocean. At our pool where my mother swims, I never go unless she makes me. Then I stay near the fence real far away from the water. I scream when she pulls me to the pool. I get sick and vomit too.

I am afraid of being in a boat in deep water. One reason is my father always trys to scare me by almost turning the boat over. But I am a good swimmer and love to fish. The only thing I think I could do about it is face it and go out in a boat, and make it turn over close to shore and get back on.

Frankenstein movies I love. Count Dracula
and vampires I love too. They are real fun. I
get super scared from them, but I like them
anyway. I get real bad dreams that are so alive,
they wake me up.

When I was a baby, I was afraid of dogs. Also loud noises, especially thunder claps, scared me like mad when I was little. When I was five there were many things that scared me. I was afraid of being in the dark by myself. To help from being scared, I'd whistle or hum. When I was six I hated big dogs and loud noises. And I used to be scared to go to bed. I used to think there was a monster under my bed that would come up and eat me. But if I put my covers over me, I would be protected from the monster. I did that until I was nine.

When I was ten we moved into a new house. When I went to bed in that house, I heard a lot of creaking noises. Every time I heard noises, it sounded like someone was walking in the house. That doesn't scare me anymore. Even now I'm scared of roller coasters and high ferris wheels. But with most of my fears I get over them.

ACKNOWLEDGEMENTS

We want to thank the 1500 boys and girls in the United States and the British West Indies who wrote essays about fear for ROBBERS, BONES & MEAN DOGS. Although only segments from selected papers were used, your help was essential. Because you shared your scary feelings openly, many other kids will learn that they have the same fears and that it is okay to be afraid.

We also wish to extend our appreciation to the following teachers for their help: Joan Boysen, Elmera Dawson, Mildred Dobson, Joyce Ephraim, Anne Garrett, Kathleen Hauser, Flora Jackson, Joanne Lonergan, Irma Moke, Margaret Newhall, and Patricia Smith.

Principals at several schools actively participated in this project by exploring the emotion of fear and coordinating the efforts of their staffs. We were especially pleased that most of the principals incorporated our project into their schools' teaching program. We wish to thank Albert Fortune, Principal, Commonwealth Christian School, Fairfax, Virginia; Joyce Goodman, Principal, Congressional Schools, Falls Church, Virginia; Thomas B. Lyles, Principal, Wakefield Forest Elementary School, Fairfax, Virginia; Obed McF. Malone, Headmaster, East End Primary, Tortola, British Virgin Islands; Peter M. Manno, Principal, Oak View Elementary School, Fairfax, Virginia; Winston A. Rhymer, Principal, St. Mary's School, Virgin Gorda, British Virgin Islands.

Ray Broekel, former Editor-in-Chief of the juvenile division at Addison-Wesley Publishing Company, receives our sincere appreciation. Without his vision and encouragement this book might never have been written.

Richard Berkey, the authors' research and public relations assistant, earns our gratitude, particularly for his efforts at the schools in the British West Indies.

Velma and Barry Berkey have authored eight books for children and adults, as well as several dozen articles in professional journals and popular magazines. *Robbers, Bones* & *Mean Dogs* is their third book on children's emotions. The Berkeys drew upon their background in education and psychiatry to create this book.

Dr. and Mrs. Berkey live with their three children in the metropolitan Washington, D.C. area.

Marylin Hafner has illustrated eighteen books for children and is a frequent contributor to *Cricket Magazine.* She was chosen to illustrate *Robbers, Bones* & *Mean Dogs* because of her inimitable witty drawings. She says she is scared of centipedes, people who slam doors and very high places.